What Do We Know About Alien Abduction?

by Kirsten Mayer

illustrated by Tim Foley

Penguin Workshop

To Mulder and Scully—KM

For Bud—TF

PENGUIN WORKSHOP
An imprint of Penguin Random House LLC, New York

First published in the United States of America by Penguin Workshop,
an imprint of Penguin Random House LLC, New York, 2023

Copyright © 2023 by Penguin Random House LLC

Penguin supports copyright. Copyright fuels creativity, encourages diverse voices, promotes free speech, and creates a vibrant culture. Thank you for buying an authorized edition of this book and for complying with copyright laws by not reproducing, scanning, or distributing any part of it in any form without permission. You are supporting writers and allowing Penguin to continue to publish books for every reader.

PENGUIN is a registered trademark and PENGUIN WORKSHOP is a trademark of Penguin Books Ltd. WHO HQ & Design is a registered trademark of Penguin Random House LLC.

Visit us online at penguinrandomhouse.com.

Library of Congress Cataloging-in-Publication Data is available.

Printed in the United States of America

ISBN 9780593387559 (paperback)   10 9 8 7 6 5 4 3 2 1 WOR
ISBN 9780593387566 (library binding)   10 9 8 7 6 5 4 3 2 1 WOR

The publisher does not have any control over and does not assume any responsibility for author or third-party websites or their content.

Contents

What Do We Know About
 Alien Abduction? 1
When Did We First See Alien Life-Forms? . . 4
The Betty and Barney Hill Case 14
Missing for Five Days 34
The Visitors Arrive 42
What Happens During
 an Alien Abduction? 55
Extraterrestrials On-Screen 66
Looking for Proof 80
The Truth Is Out There 93
Timelines 104
Bibliography 106

What Do We Know About Alien Abduction?

Betty and Barney Hill had already been married for over a year when they went on their first vacation to Niagara Falls, New York. Late in the evening of September 19, 1961, they were driving home to New Hampshire, expecting to arrive around 2:30 or 3:00 a.m. Looking out the car window, Betty watched a light in the clear, dark sky. It appeared to be moving, tracking their path closely. Was it a plane? Or something more mysterious?

When the light passed over their vehicle, just one hundred feet above the road, they stopped the car in shock. The brightly lit object appeared to be a large disk shaped like a pancake, with small, fin-shaped wings on each side and large windows across the front edge. As Barney Hill got out of the car with his binoculars, the disk floated over to a field next to the road. He approached and looked closer. He could see figures moving in the windows. One of them turned to look at him. It wasn't a human face.

Suddenly very afraid, Barney ran back to the car. But as they drove off, Betty and Barney heard unusual noises, similar to electronic beeps. When they finally got home, both of the Hills felt strange. It was 5:00 a.m., much later than they had expected it to be. They hadn't encountered any traffic or other delays. So what happened during those missing hours?

Betty and Barney sat down and drew what they could remember of the ship they had seen. Although they worked separately, their drawings of the flying disk were eerily similar. It was unlike anything they had ever encountered before, and they were not sure what to think.

What happened to the Hills that night? Would Betty and Barney ever really know?

CHAPTER 1
When Did We First See Alien Life-Forms?

Alien creatures are considered by many people to be simply myths and stories, yet they are very real to those who claim to have seen and communicated with them. These beings from another world are most often called "aliens" or sometimes even "little green men." A more accurate term is "extraterrestrial." This word means they are not from this planet.

There is a long history of humans telling stories of seeing gods, angels, and other creatures, which some have interpreted to be about extraterrestrials. Theories about ancient aliens, also called ancient astronauts, claim that these extraterrestrials came to Earth thousands of years ago and shared advanced technology with humans. People who believe these theories point to certain images in ancient art that resemble unknown ships and machinery as proof that the planet was visited by alien beings long ago.

Sightings of Unidentified Flying Objects (UFOs), now also sometimes referred to as Unidentified Aerial Phenomena (UAPs), have been reported in the United States since the late 1800s, with reports of "mystery airships" spotted in the skies. Sometimes occupants were spotted as well. Most famously, in 1896 a man named Colonel H. G. Shaw of Stockton, California, claimed that his horse and buggy came across a landed spacecraft. Three tall, slender beings emerged from the metallic craft and tried to force him and his traveling companion aboard.

The newspaper article detailing his story is considered the first published account of a possible alien abduction.

While UFO sightings report craft in different shapes, from tubes to triangles, perhaps the most well known is the disk-shaped craft often called a flying saucer. This term was first used in June 1947 by a newspaper reporting a story about a private pilot named Kenneth Arnold, who saw nine disk-shaped objects flying at high speeds near Mount Rainier, Washington.

Just a month later, the famous Roswell incident occurred, when strange debris found in a New Mexico field prompted one of the biggest controversies in American history. The United States government said it was a weather balloon that had crashed. But early news reports and later eyewitness stories claimed it was a flying saucer and its extraterrestrial crew of alien beings.

Modern reports of UFOs and alien life-forms come from all over the world. One of the first documented claims of an alien abduction was in

South America. Antônio Villas Boas said he was taken from his farm in Brazil on October 15, 1957. That night, a bright light in the sky flew toward him. When it got closer, it looked like an egg-shaped craft spinning in the air.

Strange beings came out and carried him into the ship. He described them as five feet tall, wearing gray uniforms and helmets.

After he was let off the ship and it flew away, Mr. Villas Boas realized he had been gone for over four hours. He suffered from various medical issues afterward, and a doctor convinced him to tell his story to the public in February 1958.

Antônio Villas Boas

It was difficult to believe his strange encounter, but Antônio Villas Boas wouldn't be the only person claiming to be an alien abductee for long.

Close Encounters

When a person witnesses a UFO, it is often referred to as a "close encounter." The initial system of classification for these encounters was developed by the astronomer J. Allen Hynek in 1972 and later expanded on by other ufologists (say: yoo-FAH-luh-jists), the researchers who study UFO sightings and alien encounters.

- Nocturnal Lights: A sighting of lights in the night sky
- Daylight Disk: A UFO sighting that occurs during the day

- **Radar-Visual:** A sighting that is supported by confirmation of the object on a radar device
- **Close Encounter of the First Kind:** A sighting of a UFO at close range (within five hundred feet), where details can be observed
- **Close Encounter of the Second Kind:** An encounter with a UFO in which physical effects are observed, such as when traces are left on the ground, a vehicle or electronic device stops working, or a witness experiences physical sensations
- **Close Encounter of the Third Kind:** A UFO encounter in which occupants of the craft are present and observed by witnesses
- **Close Encounter of the Fourth Kind:** A human is abducted or taken aboard a UFO
- **Close Encounter of the Fifth Kind:** Direct communication between an alien life-form and a human

CHAPTER 2
The Betty and Barney Hill Case

Betty and Barney Hill are considered the model example for modern alien abduction cases. Barney Hill was an army veteran, a postal service worker, and a Boy Scout leader. His wife, Betty,

Betty and Barney Hill

was a social worker. They lived in Portsmouth, New Hampshire. When they took their dog, Delsey, along with them in the car for a family vacation to Niagara Falls in 1961, the Hills had no idea how much their lives were about to change.

Delsey

Late in the evening on September 19, the Hills were driving home under a bright moon. Both Jupiter and Saturn were visible in the clear sky as Betty Hill looked out the car window. She noticed a light in the sky that appeared to be moving. She pointed it out to her husband,

and he guessed it could be a satellite—a machine that is launched into space to collect information or to transmit communications.

When they pulled over to let the dog out, they looked at the object through binoculars. It appeared to be some sort of craft with flashing lights.

Back in the car, the Hills thought it was following them. They wondered if it was a plane, but they couldn't hear an engine. The mysterious craft suddenly flew over their car, about one hundred feet above the road. The Hills stopped again, and it moved over to a field.

It was round, with two rows of large, rectangular windows. Barney could see several figures through his binoculars. They were wearing black and moving around inside. One of them turned and appeared to be looking right at him!

Suddenly scared, Barney ran back to the car, and the couple sped off toward their home in Portsmouth. From inside their vehicle, the Hills heard two sets of strange noises, which they later described as a series of electronic beeps. They felt strange and disoriented.

The Hills pulled into their driveway just after 5:00 a.m. It had taken them hours longer to reach home than it should have. They were unsettled. They looked at their car and found shiny, polished-looking circles on the trunk. When they held a compass over the marks, the needle spun wildly. There was other physical evidence that something had happened to them. The strap on their binoculars was broken. The zipper on Betty's dress was broken, too. Barney had unexplained scratches on the tops of his shoes. Both wore wristwatches that had stopped working (and never worked again). All these things suggested *something* had happened to them . . . but what?

Betty Hill called her sister to talk about the experience. Her sister suggested they report it to the local air force base, which the Hills did on September 21. A report was filed, but they

never heard anything more from the air force. The couple found contact information for the National Investigations Committee on Aerial Phenomena (NICAP) in Washington, DC, and informed them next. NICAP conducted multiple interviews over time and wrote reports about what the Hills had seen, which eventually became great resources for other UFO researchers.

Not quite two weeks after the encounter, Betty Hill had recurring dreams for five nights straight. She dreamed of hearing the first set of beeps, then being taken aboard an alien ship, having tests performed on her, and communicating with alien beings before being taken back to the car. Then she heard the second set of beeps. Her husband did not have any similar dreams, and at first refused to consider Betty's dreams might be anything more than that, but Betty was shaken. Had they been abducted by alien beings? Were these dreams really memories?

Eventually it was suggested to the couple that they undergo hypnosis to try to remember more.

The Hills found a respected doctor in Boston who agreed to treat them at the beginning of 1964, and each underwent hypnosis in separate sessions. Both remembered that alien beings were standing in the road before approaching the car. The beings took them into the craft while their dog was left in the car. Both Hills recalled being taken aboard the disk-shaped craft and put in separate rooms. Barney remembered the aliens using telepathy (speaking to him through thoughts) and telling him he would not be harmed. The alien beings took hair samples and fingernail clippings, and gave them something like medical exams. Barney recalled the aliens being surprised by his dentures—that he had fake teeth.

What Is Hypnosis?

Hypnosis is the process of guiding someone into an altered state, almost like a waking dream, in which they are alert and talking, but are asked to relive a memory or explore their own thoughts. While under hypnosis a person may not be fully in control of themselves and may instead follow any directions given to them.

While rooted in older traditions such as meditation, during the 1800s, hypnosis developed into a practice used by medical doctors and psychoanalysts—those who help patients tap into their unconscious minds. The famous doctor Sigmund Freud believed that it was possible to use hypnosis to help a person recall memories they had forgotten or mentally "blocked."

Once considered very effective, most scientists now consider any memories "recovered" under hypnosis to be false creations of suggestive, imaginative minds. However, hypnosis is still used therapeutically, similarly to meditation and other mindfulness practices, to reduce stress or to help break bad habits like smoking.

Hypnosis became a very popular tool used to investigate alien abductions, and many experiencers choose to go through hypnosis sessions to recall the full details of what happened to them.

While the memories Betty Hill recovered under hypnosis were similar to her nightmares, some of the details were not exactly the same. She claimed there were multiple alien beings in the room with her, and one seemed to be the leader. She could also understand what the being was saying to her, and they had a conversation. She asked to take a book from the room, but she was not allowed to. Betty asked where the beings were from and the leader let her look at a star map—a holographic projection of circles, representing stars and planets, and connecting lines, representing routes of travel. After the hypnosis session, she was able to draw the star map and some of the symbols she had seen in the book.

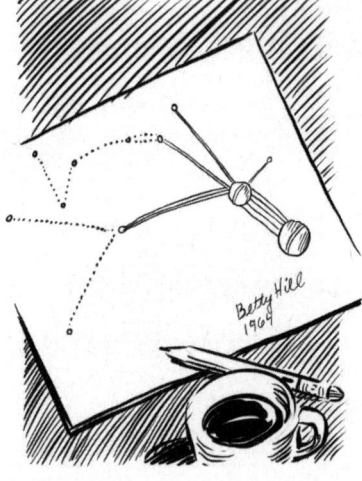

The leader told Betty Hill that neither she nor her husband would remember what had happened to them. Barney Hill was already back in the car with Delsey when Betty returned. They watched the disk lift off and disappear. They began to drive and then heard the second set of beeping tones. And that is where their conscious memories took over again.

Not everyone believed the Hills' story. Barney himself was initially afraid to admit the truth, as he had always found such things hard to believe, but the Hills decided that these recovered memories were the true account of what had happened to them. And no one else ever presented them with a better explanation.

When a book about their story called *The Interrupted Journey: Two Lost Hours "Aboard a Flying Saucer"* was published, it included the sketches they had made, both their early ones of

the ship and the later ones drawn during hypnosis. Many readers found these drawings convincing, especially the star map.

People who doubt the Hills' story have pointed out that Barney Hill's memories under hypnosis may have been based on his wife's earlier nightmares. And that Betty Hill may have seen a television program that influenced her description of the aliens. Yet it does seem that *something* happened to the couple late that night on a lonely road, when they seem to have been missing for hours. If not an alien abduction, then what?

The Hills' story was the first widely reported account of an alien abduction in the United States. Despite their fame, the Hills lived relatively normal lives afterward. Barney Hill died in 1969, and Betty Hill lived until 2004. She gave lectures and shared her story with many others throughout the rest of her life. Interest continued, and a second book cowritten by their niece was published in 2007, titled *Captured! The Betty and Barney Hill UFO Experience*.

Experiencer or Abductee?

For many years, people like the Hills were referred to as "abductees," as these incidents were commonly called "alien abductions." But as more and more people have come forward to report similar experiences, the word *experiencer* has been

adopted as a preferred term. Some experiencers report choosing to go with the alien beings aboard their craft, so in those cases, the idea that they were abducted—or taken—is not true. The word *experiencer* can also apply to anyone who reports *any* sort of contact or encounter with an alien being.

In October 1975, a film about their story, *The UFO Incident*, aired on television. Over the next few years, dozens more Americans would come forward, many more than before. In fact, one of the most well-known encounters occurred just two weeks after *The UFO Incident* was broadcast.

CHAPTER 3
Missing for Five Days

Travis Walton was a forestry worker in Snowflake, Arizona. On November 5, 1975, Travis and a crew of six other men were working to clear out undergrowth on a hundred acres of land. They worked until sunset. Just after dark, driving home in the crew leader's truck, all of the men witnessed a bright light behind a hill up ahead of them. They drove closer and a large golden disk appeared. The driver stopped the truck, and Travis hopped out to get a better look. He ran toward the craft, stopping almost directly underneath it. The men watched as the flying disk projected a bright beam of light at Travis and lifted him up into the air. He was about a foot off the ground before he fell, unconscious and unresponsive to their cries, lying underneath what appeared to be an alien ship.

Panicked and worried for their friend, the men drove to the next town and called the police for help. The deputy sheriff doubted their story, but he took a few officers and most of the workers to look for Travis, while a few of the other men from the crew went to alert family and friends.

There was nothing at the site—no Travis Walton and no sign of the disk-shaped craft. Everyone was worried, and by the next morning the police began to suspect the crew had made up the story. In the days that followed, news reporters came to the town and interviewed everyone involved. The media coverage caused a lot of suspicion. Travis's brother told reporters that they had always been interested in UFOs, and that he knew Travis would run to investigate if he ever saw one. After hearing this, the police thought it was a prank being played by the Walton brothers on the work crew, using lights and balloons to create a UFO-like scene.

On November 10, all the workers took lie detector tests to prove they did not know where Travis was, and that they were telling the truth about what they had witnessed. That night, five days after he went missing, Travis Walton finally reappeared.

He said he woke up by the side of a road and watched the craft leave. He recognized the area and walked to town to use a payphone to call his sister. When his family picked him up, he told them that he had been aboard a ship with alien beings.

He described the beings as short and bald, with white skin and large eyes. He thought he had been gone for only a few hours—he had no idea it had been five days.

Travis Walton remembered that after the light had knocked him out, he woke up in what felt like a hospital room with three of the alien beings, who were wearing orange jumpsuits. He jumped up and tried to fight them, but he was too weak to do more than swing his arms. Lights appeared, and it looked as if he was in some sort of planetarium, with a star map projected around him.

Next, he saw a different type of figure—a being about his height, with blond hair and large golden eyes, wearing a blue jumpsuit and a glass helmet. The being led him into another large room where there were three others like it, and a mask was put over Travis's face—and then he woke up by the side of the road.

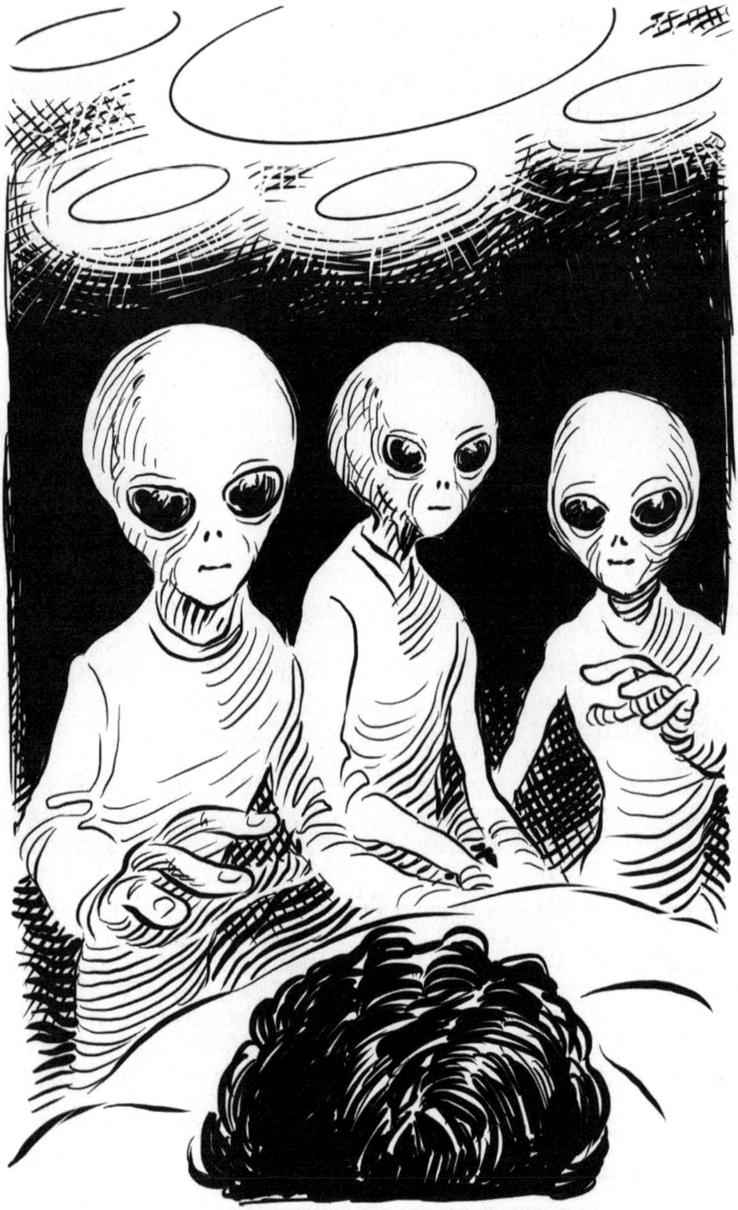

He cooperated with medical exams and lie detector tests, and underwent hypnosis to try to remember more of his experience. Many did not believe him, and the press coverage speculated that it was a hoax (an intentional prank or scam), or that his work friends had made up the story.

Betty and Barney Hill only experienced a few missing hours, but Travis Walton went through a much longer ordeal. He wrote a book about his experiences, and years later, in 1993, a movie was made based on his story. He has never wavered in what he believes happened to him, and he still gives interviews about his experience.

CHAPTER 4
The Visitors Arrive

As more and more people told abduction stories, appeared in the news, and had their stories retold in books and films, the idea of extraterrestrials taking human beings onto flying saucers became more accepted. Some people believed the events were mysteries that were simply not yet understood. In 1987, an author named Whitley Strieber published a book titled *Communion: A True Story*, in which he recounted his own alien abduction story.

Whitley and his wife and young son split their

Whitley Strieber

time between an apartment in New York City and a log cabin in upstate New York. It was the night after Christmas 1985, when he had a very strange experience at the family's cabin. After going to bed, he claims he awoke suddenly to a whooshing noise coming from the living room downstairs. He checked the burglar alarms on the house from a panel near his bed, and everything seemed fine. Then he noticed that the door to his bedroom was moving. Incredibly, he saw a small figure slowly peering around the bedroom door at him. Three and a half feet tall, small and slender, the being had two dark eyes and a small mouth. It was wearing a hat or helmet and a plate over its chest. The figure rushed toward him, and Whitley lost consciousness.

Initially, his memories of what happened came in brief flashes. The next thing he was aware of was being moved—his body was being floated or carried out of the room. He felt paralyzed, as if he were frozen into position. Next, he was aware of being outside in the woods. There were two beings nearby. One was wearing a gray jumpsuit, and Whitley felt as if the being were trying to explain something to him. Then he was floating above the trees and lowered through a gray circular opening into a room.

It was a round room with a domed ceiling, and Whitley was seated on a bench against the wall. Several small beings began rushing about, moving very fast. He recalled later that they smelled something like cinnamon. And he saw more than one kind of being. The shorter ones he had seen outside, and another being who was about five feet tall, with huge, angled black eyes, unlike the smaller round eyes of the others.

They put Whitley on a table in another room and conducted medical tests, and he remembered something being implanted in his body. They showed him a device he did not recognize, pricked his finger, and the next thing he knew he was waking up back in his own bed.

The local newspaper reported that many people in the area had seen objects with lights flying through the sky, including right near the Striebers' cabin, in late December.

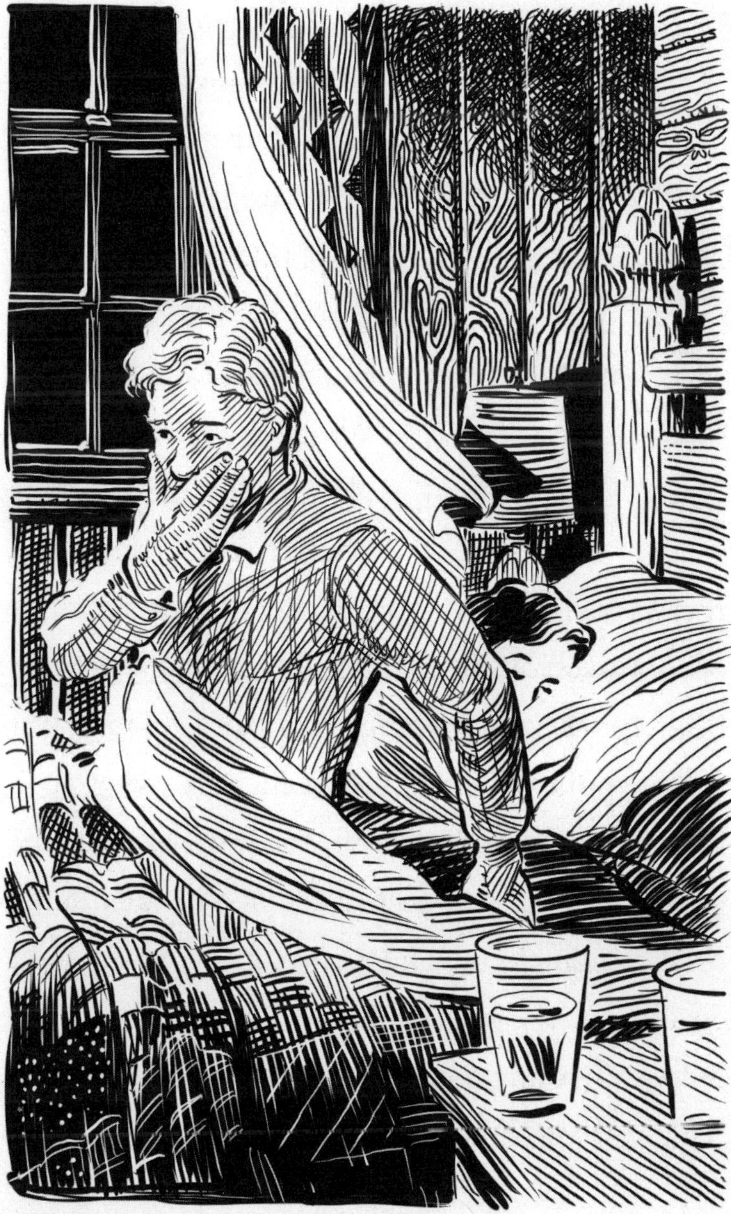

Budd Hopkins

Whitley had a lot of questions about what had happened to him, so he went to see Budd Hopkins, a ufologist and expert in abductions who happened to work near Whitley's apartment in New York City. Hopkins interviewed him and then asked if there had been any prior strange occurrences. Whitley remembered that there had been another very strange night in October, just a few months before his abduction, when two friends were staying with the Striebers at the cabin. They all had been awakened in the middle of the night by a loud bang and a bright light coming in the windows from outside. Whitley's wife and young son remembered the same loud bang waking them up.

When Whitley later asked, their friends did remember looking out the window, thinking it was bright as daylight outside, and hearing scampering feet upstairs. One friend also recalled Whitley saying that a spaceship had come to visit them, but he did not remember saying that. Each person had dismissed the event as a strange dream at the time. Looking back, though, they realized that they had experienced something together. But what?

Whitley and his wife underwent hypnosis and remembered many more details about these two nights. Whitley had never believed in anything like UFOs before, but now he dedicated himself to researching everything about them. His book *Communion* was a best seller and was made into a movie. The life-form he described was illustrated on the cover of the book, becoming a famous image that continues to be associated with extraterrestrials.

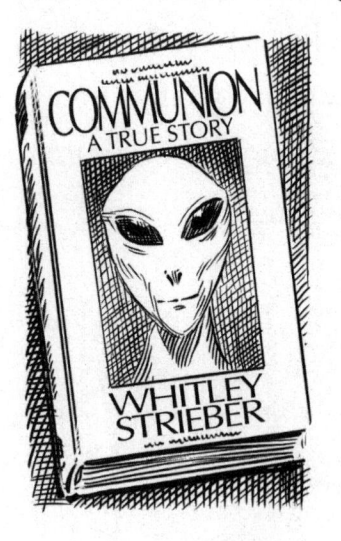

And yet Whitley was not convinced the beings that he encountered were from another planet. He referred to them as "visitors." He wondered if they could be another form of humans, from the future, or a different dimension. Or maybe, he thought, they've always been here, and could be linked to myths about other mysterious creatures like fairies.

After *Communion* was published, Whitley received letters from all around the world. He and his book were often mentioned in news stories about alien abduction

Fairy

experiences, with many public figures questioning if the reports were true. While he tried to take a scientific approach to his experiences, and never claimed to know exactly what had happened or who these beings were, Whitley was publicly called a fraud in the media.

Angels or Aliens?

There are some experiencers who believe that alien beings are actually angels, as described in the Jewish, Christian, and Islamic faiths. In the 1500s, a Spanish noblewoman called Teresa of Ávila became a nun in the Catholic Church. She claimed to have visions, and that she encountered an angel who pierced her heart with a golden lance (a long spear). Some have interpreted this as an early encounter with an alien being.

Representatives of the Catholic Church have said the church sees no conflict with its beliefs and the possible existence of alien life-forms. The Vatican has its own observatory whose astronomers hold regular meetings with scientists to explore the possibility of extraterrestrial life.

After her death in 1582, Teresa of Ávila was canonized by the Catholic Church as a saint.

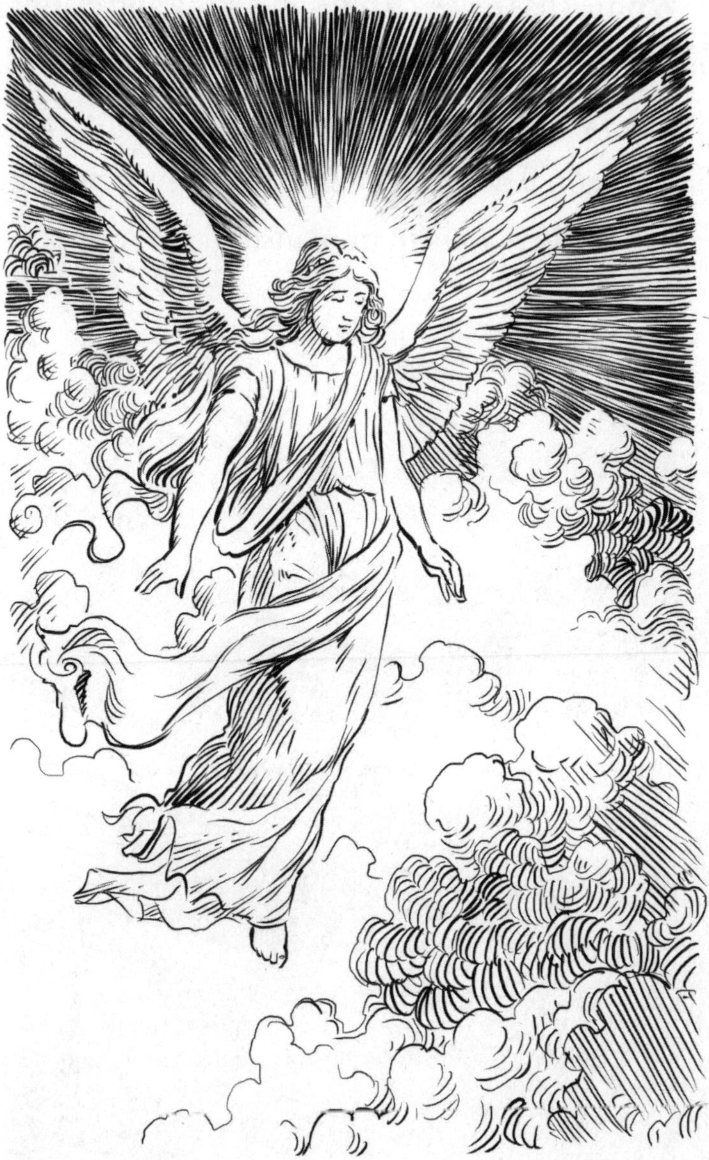

Whitley has never changed his story and claims to still have communications and experiences with the visitors. He has written dozens of books about them. And he has come to believe that the visitors are here to help humans.

CHAPTER 5
What Happens During an Alien Abduction?

Each experiencer's recounting of their story is unique in its combination of elements. They see different kinds of spacecraft with different interior rooms, and interact with different types of beings. However, there are many common elements to the experiences and certain details that many stories share.

Where and when do the encounters happen? Most often, they happen at night. Many people report being awoken in their own bed, while others report being outside in unpopulated areas. They may be driving a car or camping in a field. There are usually no witnesses beyond their own companions. They see a strange light and usually an alien craft unlike any known plane or jet.

Many don't recall the full abduction experience right away. They will remember seeing the UFO and maybe even an alien being, but then their memory will jump ahead to the end of the experience. They know that time has passed, often hours or even days, but they can't yet remember what happened during that time. This is referred to as "missing time."

Clocks or watches around them may stop working during the experience. There may also be things wrong with their clothes—they are on backward, or a zipper is broken, little details that show that something has happened. And they don't always return to the same place they were abducted from. For example, they may go to sleep in their bedroom, but wake up in the backyard.

As more detailed memories return, many experiencers recall actually going aboard an alien ship. They may be "beamed" aboard by a beam of light that pulls them in. Or they are simply floated through the air. Some even experience moving through solid items like a closed door or a wall.

While most people are familiar with the image of a gray alien with a pear-shaped, bald head and huge black eyes, experiencers report meeting different kinds of beings, and often there are two different types of life-forms aboard the ship with them. Some are described as "workers" who bring the experiencer aboard and do small tasks, and then there are others described as "leaders," or sometimes "doctors," who are usually the beings who can communicate with humans.

Gray alien

Sometimes experiencers report hearing the extraterrestrials communicate with sounds they can't understand, and others recall being able to send and receive messages through their thoughts—this is called telepathy. Many say they were shown images, almost like movies, to indicate warnings about the future of Earth.

Types of Extraterrestrial Craft

Experiencers and other UFO eyewitnesses have described seeing a variety of unidentified craft in the skies. These are the shapes most often reported.

- **Flying Saucer or Disk:** The famous round, spinning crafts have been seen in a variety of shapes and configurations. The Hills saw a round, flat ship with two rows of windows. The Gulf Breeze photographs that experiencer Ed Walters took show a taller craft with a narrower top and bottom, and a round light shining from the bottom.

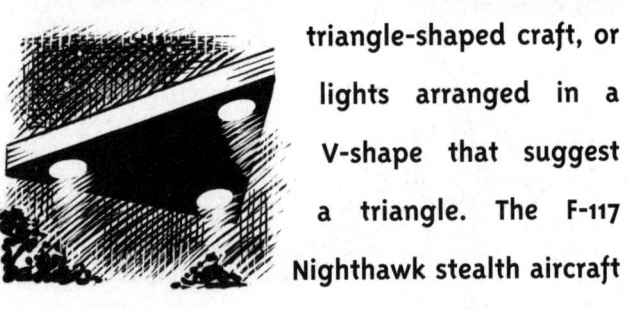

- **Triangle or Boomerang:** Reports often feature triangle-shaped craft, or lights arranged in a V-shape that suggest a triangle. The F-117 Nighthawk stealth aircraft was secretly flown over Area 51 for years before being revealed to the public, and critics argue that these planes are what were seen. Others counter these tests can't account for all the sightings across the United States and Europe that continue to this day.

- Cylindrical: Other sightings describe an elongated, slender shape with rounded ends, like a sausage. Perhaps the most well-known sighting is a video showing an unidentified object filmed by a US Navy pilot in November 2004. The witnesses described the mysterious object as being shaped like a Tic Tac candy.

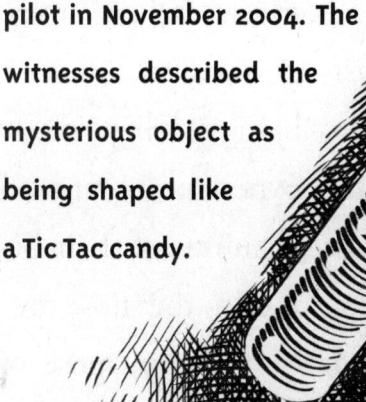

Almost all experiencers believe they went through some sort of medical exam or test conducted by alien beings. They might take hair or skin samples. Experiencers report having implants put into or taken out of their bodies—small metal objects put in the nose or under the skin. It's unclear what the purpose of these implants might be.

Different reasons are given for these exams. Many think these beings are studying humans to learn more about our species, the same way we study animals in the wild. Others believe they are trying to create alien-human hybrids, creatures who would be part alien being, part human.

A few experiencers even claim to have been shown hybrid children. Some think this is an attempt to save either humans or the alien species from extinction. These types of stories have been the basis for many TV shows and films.

Many experiencers who come forward later report that they have continued to encounter alien beings, and may even eventually recall other experiences that happened when they were younger. The repeat abductions often accompany increasing and ongoing communication with the aliens.

Having such a strange experience is scary for most people. Many experiencers have a difficult time understanding how such an extraordinary thing could happen in their life. Of those who have repeat experiences, many often come to see these visits as positive events and may view the alien life-forms as well-intentioned beings who are trying to help humankind.

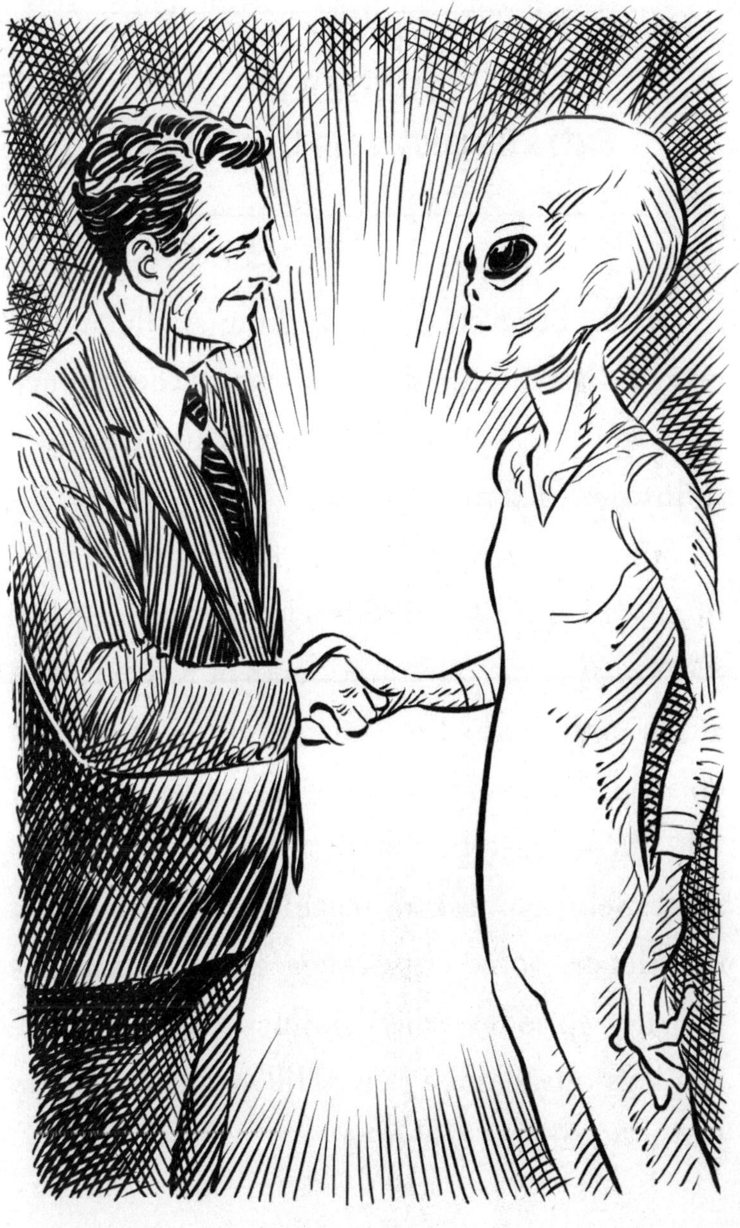

CHAPTER 6
Extraterrestrials On-Screen

While believers were working to document and understand the stories of those who claimed to have been abducted, the movie and television industries tried to keep up.

Some researchers trace the first representation of a "gray" alien to a 1960s television series called *The Outer Limits*, several episodes of which feature aliens and abduction stories. One particular episode, "The Bellero Shield," aired February 10, 1964—just before Barney and Betty Hill underwent hypnosis to regain memories of their experience. Some critics suggest the appearance of the episode's alien influenced the Hills' recollections, despite Betty Hill's claims that they had not watched the show.

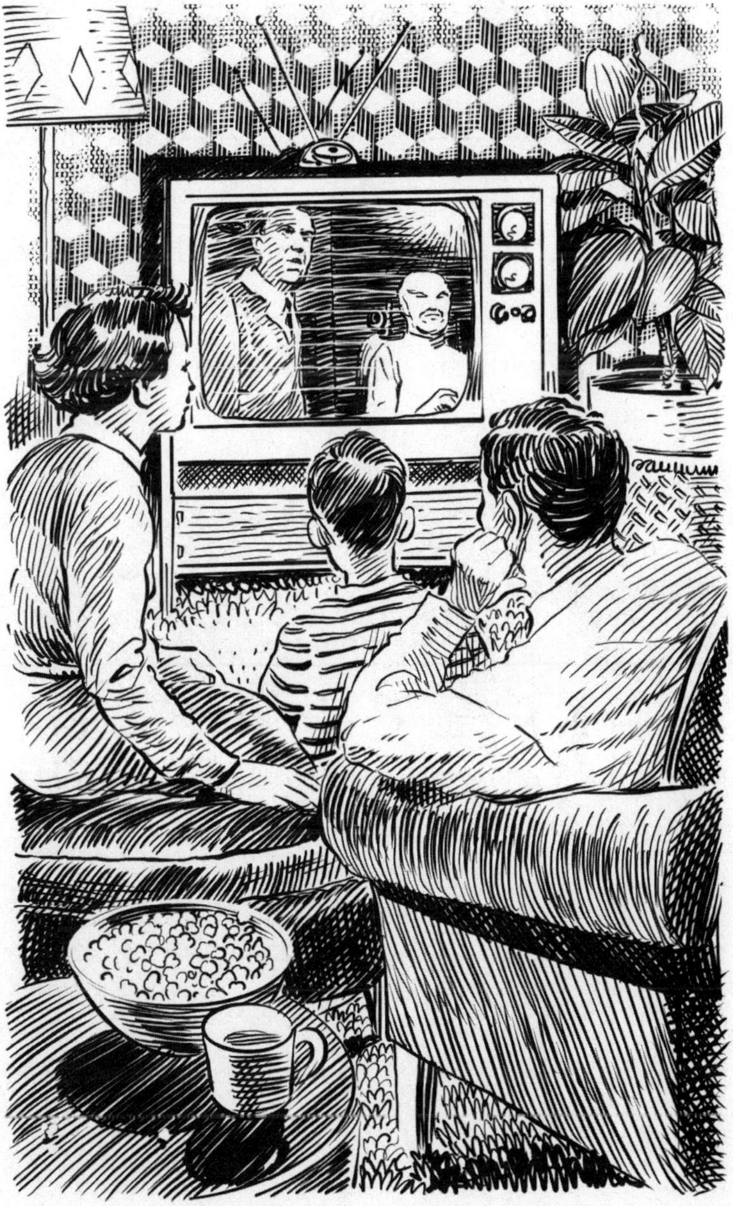

Interest in UFOs and alien visitation greatly increased after the publication of the 1968 book *Chariots of the Gods?* and the related documentary film. Author Erich von Däniken thought that ancient structures like the pyramids in Egypt and the Nazca Lines in Peru must have been built with the help of alien technology. He didn't believe that humans could have accomplished these amazing things themselves. He also popularized the idea that some cultures' ancient art showed extraterrestrial beings and spacecraft. While many historians and scientists have dismissed his claims, the book captured the public's imagination. In the title, Däniken is asking if technology and religion could have been brought to Earth by alien astronaut gods. The alleged "proof" for his ideas can be seen today in the television series *Ancient Aliens*.

Other films that made big impressions include the box-office hit and award-winning film *Close Encounters of the Third Kind*, which appeared in theaters in 1977. Director Steven Spielberg consulted astronomer and ufologist J. Allen Hynek on the story, and the film's plot, although fictional, featured many common elements from experiencers' actual abduction stories. So much so, perhaps, that the air force and the National Aeronautics and Space Administration (NASA) refused to cooperate with the filming of *Close Encounters*, and NASA reportedly objected to its release. This film helped popularize the idea that the alien beings come in peace.

Extraterrestrials were shown as being even more family friendly with two films in the 1980s: the 1982 film *E.T. the Extra-Terrestrial* and the 1986 film *Flight of the Navigator*.

In *E.T.*, another blockbuster directed by Steven Spielberg, a gentle alien lands on Earth and becomes separated from its shipmates. A human boy befriends it and tries to keep the alien safe from government scientists, who want to capture it for study. It is an example of a reverse-abduction story.

In *Flight of the Navigator,* an unseen alien life-form communicates with a human boy through an intelligent spaceship, takes the boy to space, and returns him eight years later. The life-form is peaceful and only wanted to study

the boy before returning him safely home. The ship then helps the boy escape a government scientist.

Men in Black

Fans of the popular *Men in Black* movies may not realize that the original stories are based in reality.

As early as 1947, stories of mysterious men in dark suits followed UFO and alien sightings. The earliest accounts are from researchers and scientists who say the serious visitors in suits and ties ordered them to destroy their UFO files.

Other reports say the men warned experiencers to "keep quiet" or something bad might happen to them.

It is rumored that these "men in black" work for a secret US government agency trying to hide the existence of extraterrestrials. (A few even suggest they are alien beings themselves!)

But skeptics trace the spread of the men in black stories to the publication of a 1956 book called *They Knew Too Much About Flying Saucers* by Gray Barker. Many years later these stories inspired comic book author Lowell Cunningham to write a series called *The Men in Black*, which then served as the inspiration for the popular film franchise.

The idea of the government as an "enemy" enters many of these stories, first as an agency covering up the existence of alien life, and then—as seen in these last two films—as one that would imprison innocent life-forms to study them for science.

This idea of the government keeping secrets and lying about UFOs to the public came to its peak in the very popular television series and films *The X-Files*. Premiering in 1993, the show follows two FBI agents working to uncover the truth about alien life and the government cover-up of its existence. It features many different stories of alien abduction, and the main characters investigate cases that include many of the events reported in a typical abduction experience: missing time, medical tests, and implants. One of the agents, Fox Mulder, believes his missing sister was abducted by aliens when they were children, and his partner, Agent Dana Scully,

Dana Scully and Fox Mulder

is abducted herself and subjected to experiments in a story that spans several episodes of the show. The program also incorporates the idea that aliens are working with humans to create alien-human hybrids.

There are several newer television series that claim to be true stories about UFOs, alien abductions, and the truth about contact between humans and extraterrestrial beings. They reflect a renewed interest in learning more about who may or may not be visiting Earth, and how and when they arrive. Have books, movies, television shows, and mainstream news coverage on the subject influenced people's beliefs? Possibly. A poll taken in 2021 showed that 41 percent of American adults believe that some UFO sightings are alien spacecraft and cannot be explained by human activity. This is increased from 33 percent in the same poll just two years earlier!

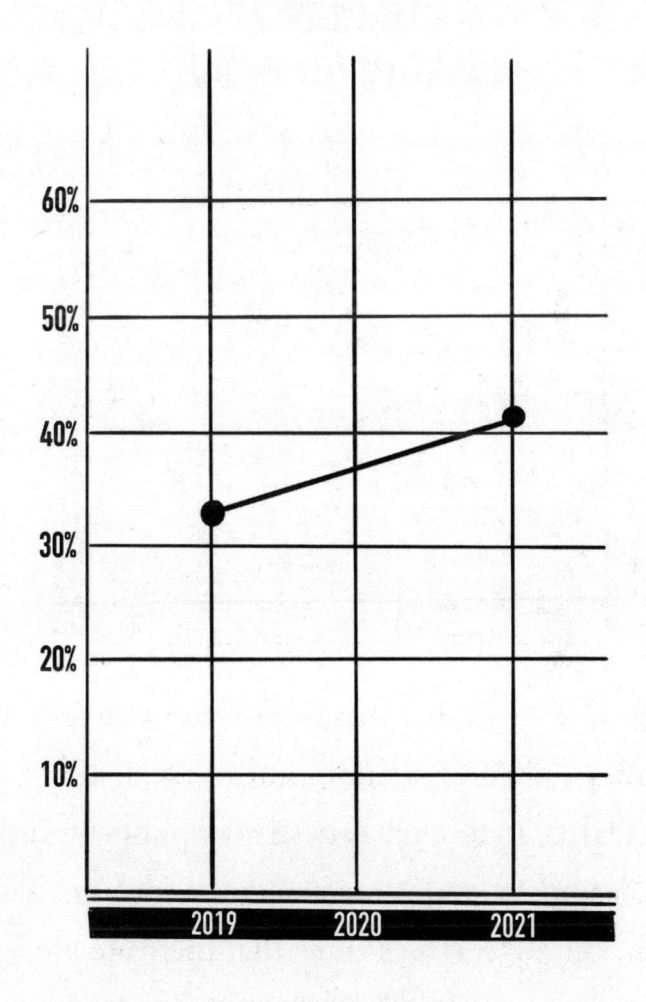

Percentage of American adults who believe that some UFOs are alien spacecraft

CHAPTER 7
Looking for Proof

How can we tell if these stories are true or not? Critics of alien abduction stories think that no one shared abduction experiences publicly until popular books and movies put the idea in their heads. But even critics agree that there are plenty of reasons to stay silent. Sharing an unusual story of alien abduction opens a person up to shame and public embarrassment. Some people feel that this is reason enough to believe such stories. Why would experiencers risk humiliation if their experiences aren't true? People who claim that they've been aboard a spaceship and have communicated with alien beings are often dismissed as liars.

Experiencers are former or active military personnel, teachers, social workers, and parents—average American citizens. Many of them find their own experiences hard to believe and are even scared of what happened. The need for an explanation is what drives many of them to seek help. They volunteer for medical exams, lie detector tests, investigations, and hypnosis in order to prove the truth of their claims. Some wait until after their careers are over to go public with their story, so that it will not damage their reputation. They do not want to risk losing their jobs or families.

Hypnosis

Researchers are interested in the mental and emotional effects of these abduction memories, and hypnosis sessions have been conducted with hundreds of experiencers to study it. Scientific studies have been written and books published on the subject. Yet it's still something that some people believe is real and others do not.

But is there proof that aliens exist? There are many photographs and videos of unidentified objects in the sky—some more detailed than others. But very few people claim to have photographed an alien being. While many of the photos are interesting, it's difficult to prove that they are "real." And there are some that have been exposed as hoaxes.

One very interesting case comes from Gulf Breeze, a small town outside Pensacola, Florida, where many sightings have been reported over the years. Starting November 11, 1987, and continuing for several months, building contractor Ed Walters and his family claimed to see UFOs, which he captured in Polaroid photographs and videos. He claimed that the alien beings repeatedly visited his home. He saw them in his yard. And they attempted to abduct him more than once by lifting him off the ground with a beam

Ed Walters

of light, which was also witnessed by his wife. On May 1, 1988, he said he experienced over an hour of missing time during a UFO craft sighting and woke up not in his truck, but on the beach nearby. He later became convinced that he had finally been taken by the beings during this time.

The Investigators

Initially, people reported sightings and experiences to local police, military bases, or government agencies. But most often these reports were met with disbelief or were ignored. Volunteer organizations were formed to investigate. These are a few of the most well-known groups:

- **Aerial Phenomena Research Organization (APRO)** ran from 1952 to 1988 and had many notable scientists and professors as consultants.
- **Center for UFO Studies (CUFOS)** was founded in 1973 by astronomer J. Allen Hynek, the creator of the "close encounter" classification system. It maintains a large archive available for study, including the files from the now-defunct NICAP.

- Mutual UFO Network (MUFON) is a nonprofit organization founded in 1969, and still actively investigates reports.

- National Investigations Committee on Aerial Phenomena (NICAP) operated as a UFO-research group from 1956 to 1980, and its board included many former military and CIA professionals.

Ed Walters submitted early photos to his local newspaper, the *Gulf Breeze Sentinel*, to be printed, and the images quickly became famous because they were some of the clearest UFO photos ever taken. He continued to share his photos and videos and was featured on the local news. Eventually he became the subject of an extensive MUFON investigation. Ed submitted to two lie detector tests to show he believed what he was saying.

Although he later published a book detailing all of his experiences, with supporting evidence and witness statements, the Walters family was accused of making up their story and faking the photos from the very beginning. Despite numerous other witnesses seeing similar UFOs in the area, the press attention focused on the Walters family.

Years later, someone moved into the house the family used to live in and claimed to find something incredible in the attic. The new owner said they found a UFO model made of Styrofoam plates and drafting paper. Using the model, debunkers (those who work to expose false claims) were able to create photos very similar to Ed Walters's images. A reporter wrote an entire book about the Walters' assumed hoax.

For his part, Ed Walters maintained that the model was put there to discredit him, and that his photographs were real. Experts have weighed in on the images and disagree on them. Some say that because of certain details there is no way they are faked, and others say it was definitely a hoax.

UFO model

But the model UFO does not exactly match the spacecraft in the photos. And Ed was far from the only person to report strange sightings in the area—hundreds of other Gulf Breeze residents reported seeing strange lights and spinning disks in the sky.

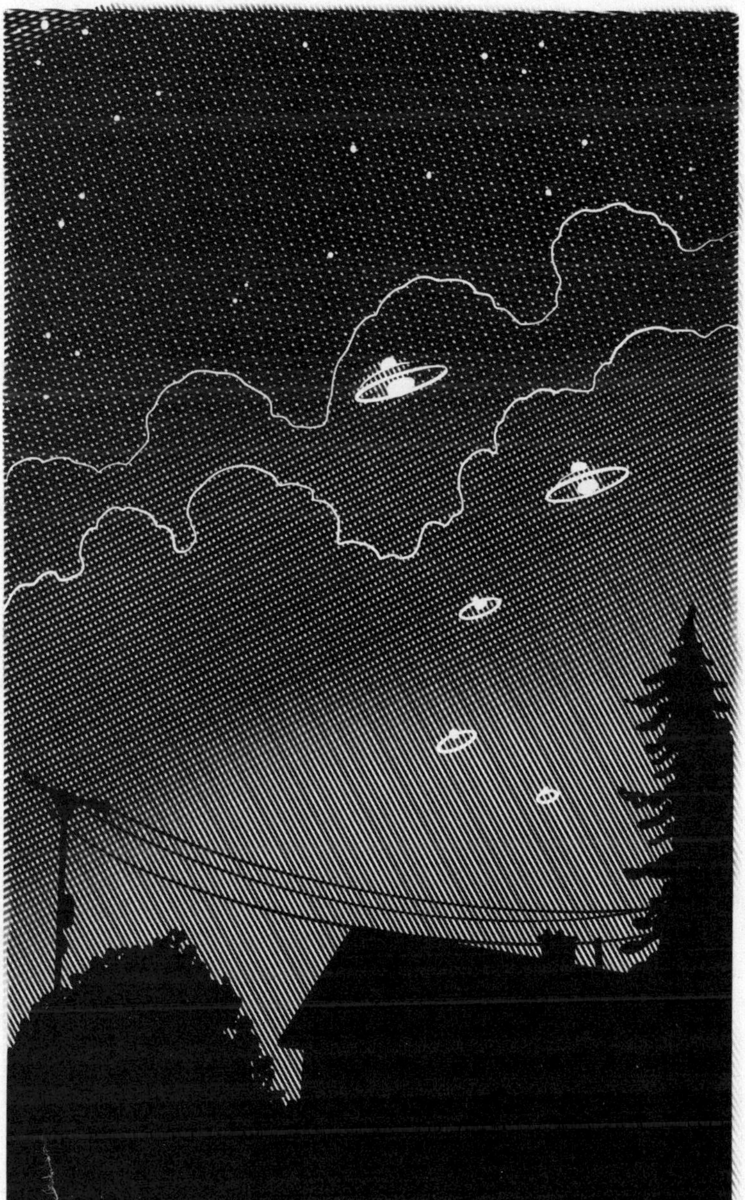

As is the case with many of these stories, there is an air force base in the Pensacola area, and Ed claimed he was threatened by "men in black" who identified themselves as being with the air force.

So he also guessed that the US government was behind the efforts to discredit his story. Why would the government ever do such a thing?

CHAPTER 8
The Truth Is Out There

What does the United States government know about extraterrestrial life? They certainly have been studying the subject for decades.

Most famously, there was a program codenamed "Project Blue Book" conducted by the US Air Force from 1952 to 1969. Blue Book picked up work from two earlier short-lived programs called Project Sign and Project Grudge, which were started as a result of multiple UFO sightings, including the Roswell incident. Blue Book's mission was to analyze data to determine if any UFOs were a threat to national security.

After several sightings over Washington, DC, in 1952, the Central Intelligence Agency (CIA) formed a panel of experts to review material from Project Blue Book. The panel concluded that the military was being overwhelmed by reports of sightings and recommended the government start a campaign to debunk the existence of UFOs through media such as educational programs, documentaries, or even cartoons. The thinking was that if they could persuade more people that UFOs didn't exist, then there would be fewer reports to follow up on. Many researchers think this suggestion from the panel is what led to the stories of "men in black." Experiencers reported being scared by people identifying themselves as government officials, who warned them away from publicly admitting they believed in UFOs or alien beings.

While not revealed to the public until 2017, Congress approved funds to study unidentified crafts from 2007 to 2012 through a secret Pentagon program called the Advanced Aerospace Threat Identification Program. This program was made public in 2017, when videos of unidentified objects seen by Navy personnel were leaked.

The government officially released those videos in 2020 and confirmed them to be real.

While the US government has always been secretive and rarely releases any information about UFOs, other governments have been more open. Official data and reports on sightings have been released by government agencies in France, Belgium, Russia, the United Kingdom, Brazil, Chile, Mexico, and Peru. Will the United States finally share more of what it knows? At the end of 2021, Congress passed a bill that includes funding to create a new office to study UFOs, or as they are now calling them, Unidentified Aerial Phenomena (UAP), meaning unidentified events that have been observed in the air. The Office of the Director of National Intelligence released a report earlier that year that stated the government had detected 143 UAPs since 2004. With astronomers now estimating there may be 300 million worlds in the Milky

Way galaxy that are capable of hosting life, who knows what this new government task force will find?

The Milky Way

A galaxy is a group of stars, planets, gas, and dust held together by gravity. The planet Earth is part of a solar system that resides within a galaxy called the Milky Way.

The Milky Way appears to be a spiral shape. The arms of the spiral are densely clustered stars. In remote areas on Earth with little artificial light, you can look up into a clear night sky and see one of these arms: a cloudy white line of stars that looks almost like milk splashed across the sky. This is where the name "milky way" comes from.

The Milky Way galaxy contains at least one hundred billion stars, most of which have at least one planet in orbit, but astronomers are still discovering more each year.

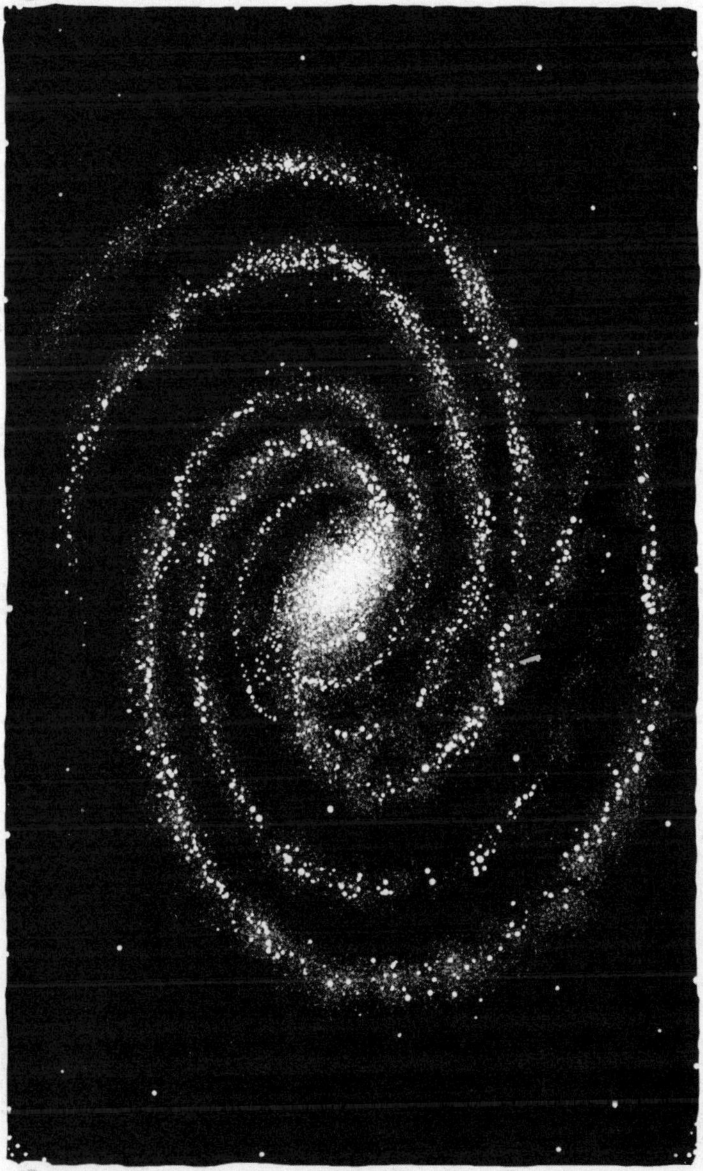

If all the experiencers who claim to have been aboard flying saucers and communicated with extraterrestrial beings are telling the truth, and if alien beings have been visiting the Earth for decades, or even thousands of years, then what do extraterrestrials want from humans?

There are a few different explanations offered by experiencers themselves. Some say these beings may be traveling from a ruined world and want to make Earth their new home.

Many repeated experiencers say that the visitors carry warnings to take better care of our own planet, and of one another. They think the extraterrestrials come in peace. These experiencers claim they have been asked to share this message, and that is one of the reasons why they choose to tell their stories.

If the Office of the Director of National Intelligence uncovers evidence of extraterrestrial life, then perhaps the truth about alien abductions can finally be revealed. The search for concrete proof continues, but believers know the truth is out there.

Timeline of Alien Abduction

- **1957** — Antônio Villas Boas of Brazil reportedly experiences an alien abduction
- **1961** — Betty and Barney Hill experience what they later believe is an alien abduction
- **1964** — *The Outer Limits* episode called "The Bellero Shield" airs on US television
- **1975** — *The UFO Incident*, a film about Betty and Barney Hill's experience, airs on television
  - Travis Walton and his coworkers see a flying saucer, and Travis is reported missing for five days
- **1977** — *Close Encounters of the Third Kind* is released in movie theaters
- **1982** — The film *E.T. the Extra-Terrestrial* premieres
- **1987** — Whitley Strieber publishes the best-selling book *Communion*, which recounts his experiences with what he calls the "visitors"
  - The *Gulf Breeze Sentinel* newspaper publishes photos of a UFO seen by Ed Walters
- **1993** — The *X-Files* television series premieres
- **2021** — The Office of the Director of National Intelligence publishes its report, *Preliminary Assessment: Unidentified Aerial Phenomena*, officially revealing US-government detected UAPs

Timeline of the World

1955	Disneyland opens in Anaheim, California
1963	Reverend Martin Luther King Jr. delivers his "I Have a Dream" speech in Washington, DC
1966	*Star Trek* premieres on television
1969	Astronauts Neil Armstrong and Edwin "Buzz" Aldrin Jr. land on the moon
1976	Apple Computer, Inc., now Apple Inc., is formed by Steve Jobs and Steve Wozniak
1989	The Berlin Wall comes down, reuniting East and West Berlin, Germany
1995	Ian Wilmut (now Sir Ian Wilmut) and a team of researchers at the Roslin Institute clone the world's first sheep
2000	Astronauts first take up residence aboard the International Space Station
2021	Beyoncé becomes the singer and the female artist with the most Grammy Awards after winning her twenty-eighth Grammy
	Around 3.89 billion people worldwide are fully vaccinated against COVID-19

Bibliography

*****Books for young readers**

Abedi, Colet, and Hugh Hardy. ***Unsealed: Alien Files***. Season 3, episode 9, "Signs of Abduction." Aired May 5, 2014, on History.

*Anderson, Clayton C. ***It's a Question of Space: An Ordinary Astronaut's Answers to Sometimes Extraordinary Questions***. Lincoln, NE: University of Nebraska Press, 2018.

Barnes, Julian E. "U.S. Can't Explain U.F.O.s, Report Says, and Doesn't Rule Out Aliens." ***New York Times***, June 26, 2021.

Birnes, William J., and Harold Burt. ***Unsolved UFO Mysteries: The World's Most Compelling Cases of Alien Encounter***. New York: Warner Books, 2000.

Clancy, Susan A. ***Abducted: How People Come to Believe They Were Kidnapped by Aliens***. Cambridge, MA: Harvard University Press, 2005.

Donderi, Don, PhD. ***UFOs, ETs, and Alien Abductions: A Scientist Looks at the Evidence***. Charlottesville, VA: Hampton Roads Publishing, 2013.

Fowler, Raymond E. ***The Andreasson Affair: The True Story of a Close Encounter of the Fourth Kind***. Pompton Plains, NJ: New Page Books, 2015.

Fuller, John G. ***The Interrupted Journey: Two Lost Hours "Aboard a Flying Saucer."*** New York: Dial Press, 1966.

Hunter, Nik. "Incident at Devils Den (part 1)." December 16, 2019. *UFO Chronicles Podcast*. Podcast. Season 1, episode 30, 1 hr., 12 min.

Lewis-Kraus, Gideon. "How the Pentagon Started Taking U.F.O.s Seriously." *New Yorker*, April 30, 2021.

Luca, Betty Andreasson, and Bob Luca. *A Lifting of the Veil*. Self-published, 2017.

Lustig, Lee, and Darcy Weir, directors. *Beyond the Spectrum: Being Taken*. 2018. 1 hr., 14 min.

Mack, John E., MD. *Abduction: Human Encounters with Aliens*. New York: Scribner, 1994.

Mazzola, Michael, director. *Unacknowledged: An Expose of the World's Greatest Secret*. Auroris Media, 2017. 1 hr., 43 min. https://www.amazon.com/dp/B06ZYGGG2N.

Monroe, Mark, director. *UFO*. Season 1, episode 4. Aired August 29, 2021, on Showtime.

Murphy, Duncan. *Close Encounters: Volume One: The Abduction Cases of Betty & Barney Hill, Travis Walton, and Antonio Villas-Boas*. Self-published, 2018.

Spanos, Nicholas P. *Multiple Identities & False Memories: A Sociocognitive Perspective*. Washington, DC: American Psychological Association, 1996.

Strieber, Whitley. ***Communion: A True Story***. New York: Harper, 2008.

Sturrock, Peter A. ***The UFO Enigma: A New Review of the Physical Evidence***. New York: Hachette Book Group, 2000.

Sweet, Tony. "What Happened at Devils Den? What is a Dream or Reality? Terry Lovelace." May 24, 2021. ***Truth Be Told Podcast***, 1 hr., 1 min.

Unidentified with Demi Lovato. Season 1, episode 1, "They Come at Night." Aired September 30, 2021, on Peacock.

Walters, Ed, and Frances Walters. ***The Gulf Breeze Sightings: The Most Astounding Multiple Sightings of UFOs in U.S. History***. New York: William Morrow, 1990.